Play On

Play On

Role of a Dementia Caregiver

Tom Cinque

ISBN: 1533137633
ISBN 13: 9781533137630

ENTRANCE

All the world's a stage,
And all the men and women merely players:
They have their exits and their entrances;
And one man in his time plays many parts…

In William Shakespeare's *As You Like It*, one of his most frequently quoted passages compares the world to a stage and life to a play. It catalogues the seven stages of a person's life, sometimes referred to as the "Seven Ages of Man": infant, schoolchild, lover, soldier, justice, pantaloon (a fool, greedy, butt of jokes), and old age (facing imminent death).

I agree with Shakespeare. On stage as a caregiver, I play the starring role in the play, and the play is called *Dementia*. Throughout the drama, I remain next to my partner during the progressive stages of my loved one's life, from the beginning of the disease to its progressive end, from its infancy to old age.

A well-known theater axiom states that despite the difficulties, "the show must go on." For a caregiver, the stages of dementia are analogous to various acts of a play. My part is to "play on" despite what challenges this role gives me.

On stage, living with the "dis-ease" imbues the caregiver with "stage fright." This book is partially a diary to expose my inner feelings and thoughts (for therapeutic reasons), and I share stories so that others know what it means to be a caregiver. Daily management of my wife's dementia has been a teachable experience for me. Hopefully, I can give a lesson to others: to those on the stage giving direct care for a loved one; to those who want to be on the main floor giving encouragement to the caregiver or patient; or to those in the balcony witnessing a friend, relative, or acquaintance in the play called *Dementia*.

Currently, the Alzheimer's Association states that this disease ranks as the sixth leading cause of death in America. One in eight older citizens has dementia. By the year 2040, twenty million people will be diagnosed with dementia (*Information and Tips for Family Care Giving*, "Alzheimer's Care," Barber Voss Home Care, 2015). Everybody will know someone stricken by this disease. By learning from caregivers, we can all manage to gracefully play our roles in the theater.

CAST

Lead Characters

My father, **Dr. Tom Cinque, MD**, loved academic medicine. After earning a degree from Fordham University, he received three rejection letters from American medical schools. Therefore, he attended medical school in Bologna, Italy, for one year. Academic success in Italy made it possible for him to transfer and complete medical school at Creighton University in Omaha, Nebraska (graduating in 1959). Specializing in internal medicine in Long Island, New York, Dad displayed a gift in diagnosing difficult cases. After twelve years working in New York, proving his talents as a teacher and administrator, he earned the position of associate dean of the medical school at Michigan State University. Ten years later, he was appointed assistant dean of the medical school at University of Nevada. Toward the end of his career, he obtained his dream job, dean of the medical school at Creighton University, the first alumnus to hold this position. He also specialized in medical ethics and taught this nationwide. Hobbies included golfing, reading, solving crossword puzzles, and watching TV.

My wife, **Sandy Cinque**, was the oldest of thirteen children and the daughter of an air force colonel. She earned her degree in botany and proved to be multitalented, displaying gifts as a seamstress (e.g., sewing her sister's wedding dress), a gardener (growing herbs, flowers, and landscaping), a cook (including food from all ethnicities), a decorator (making curtains, hanging wallpaper, creating centerpieces), a painter (enhancing rooms and canvas), a remodeler (restoring a house built in 1835), a photographer (taking pictures of nature and people), a dancer (ballet and ballroom), a trainer (all breeds of dogs), and a licensed cosmetologist (hair and skin care for thirty years). She managed two salons at the local mall and was the proprietor of Sandy's Hair and Skin Care Inc. for ten years. She created and drew the logo for the business and received a registered trademark for the design and the name of the incorporation. I jokingly stated of her numerous gifts, "She puts Martha Stewart to shame!"

Act I

The Curtain Rises on the Play

My father, Dr. Tom, was known as an educated man who spoke and read well, and he taught and talked about numerous and various disciplines. My family called him a "walking encyclopedia." (Remember that phrase? This was before Google.) In 2004, at the age of seventy-two, I found it more than strange when my father, the professor, intellectual, and leader who engaged in articulate conversations and instructions about important matters (e.g., current affairs, politics, religion, and economics) failed to complete his sentences. I began to ask myself, "Why am I completing my father's sentences when he knows more than I do?"

My family's initial assessment was, "He's getting older [in his early seventies]. Now in retirement, he's just slowing down." A few years later, my family looked back and realized that my father's difficulty with the formulation of words and sentences (called *aphasia*) was the first sign of the onset of Alzheimer's. In the beginning, my mother considered it odd that my father, who independently completed crossword puzzles, started to give the blank portions to her. This first stage of the disease began a slow deterioration that lasted nine years. On October 22, 2013, he died at the age of eighty-one.

1

My mother dedicated fifty-seven years of her life to my dad. Caring for her husband was her mission as a wife; she took "for better or worse" seriously. During the journey of caring for my father, three of my siblings and I were limited in assisting my mother because we were scattered across the United States and my older brother was in Italy. During the last five years of the disease, I flew to their home in Las Vegas one to two times per year. I clearly witnessed the steps of the deterioration during these occasional visits. By the time of his death, our family understood the disease, its stages, and its management. Therefore, to my benefit, my father, the iconic teacher, gave me my last lesson.

When I met my wife, Sandy, in 1996, she managed the salon at the local mall, having practiced cosmetology for fifteen years. She was attractive both in her appearance and in personality, and we started dating after only a few months of friendship. During our dating conversations, she frequently spoke about "the accident." On October 13, 1981, while running in a competitive event, a drunk driver hit her and three companions. She needed to be "rebuilt" (plate on her skull, spine fused together, knee replacements, facial plastic surgery, and teeth implants) due to the severity of her head injury and numerous broken bones. I noticed quirkiness due to the accident, but Sandy was still likeable, talented, and giving.

Sandy claimed her birth year as 1957, and this date was displayed on her driver's license and all documents. I didn't think that Sandy being four years older than me was a significant issue. About six months into our relationship, we took a ten-hour trip to visit her mother. On her mom's coffee table rested the family Bible. I opened the cover where her father had written the birthdays of the thirteen children. It stated Sandy's birth year as 1951, not 1957. Sandy read it and was shocked, stating that her father had made a mistake. (But the Bible does not lie!) On the drive home, she remained quiet the entire trip. Surprisingly, Sandy discovered her abusive ex-husband had set up a new birth date and a new Social Security number for her after the accident, intending to make some type of gain out of it. I pondered how the consequences of the accident created "black holes" about her past. Some of her history was a blank slate, and she needed to discover parts of her own identity.

While we were dating, Sandy's siblings told me a story. In Sandy's late teenage years, an argument with her father erupted. This led to their father slamming Sandy's head against a porcelain sink, causing unconsciousness and a concussion. Also, I heard stories from Sandy's children and siblings about the ex-husband being physically and emotionally abusive throughout their twenty-three-year marriage. The domestic violence episodes of being hit, punched, or pushed down the stairs led to numerous hospitalizations for Sandy. Additionally, she was abused in a nonphysical way. The ex-husband isolated Sandy from her immediate family by refusing visits, monitoring her phone calls, and telling her siblings lies about how badly he was being treated by her. Feeling lost and unsupported, Sandy lacked the confidence to separate from him. Also, there was the religious belief against divorce and a determination to raise her three boys with a husband. To her benefit, after twenty-three years of marriage, the ex-husband desired a divorce and organized the legal procedures. Being the victim of abuse by her father and ex-husband caused irreparable damage, but obtaining the divorce may have saved her life.

After the divorce and before the incident of Sandy discovering her true birthday, she attended training to be a flight attendant for TWA. She needed to increase her income because the divorce had left her in poverty. After she completed the course but before she started flying, TWA dismissed her due to the discrepancy in her Social Security numbers. Although she was confused about having two Social Security numbers and disappointed about being fired, Sandy remained persistently determined to rebuild her life and become independent.

After the revelation of our ten-year age difference, I weighed its significance: Should this make a difference? Is age just a number? Why is it not questioned when the man is older? My conclusion: Sandy is my best friend, and I'm in love with her. I can't change this. We exchanged marriage vows a year later, and during the first thirteen years, we shared a mutual Romeo-and-Juliet love.

Act II

True Love Means Giving

On their wedding day, when couples exchange vows, they may not truly hear the words "for worse." We may be overly optimistic—or possibly naïve—that our marriage will be always "for better." Reality is that love is not a feeling but an action; true love is not a noun but a verb. "Once loving begins to hurt is when one is starting to truly love," Mother Teresa said. In addressing the difficult times of marriage, just as in being in a caregiver role, our *actions* demonstrate our commitment to love. This truth is summed up well by Oscar Hammerstein:

> *A bell's not a bell 'til you ring it,*
> *A song's not a song 'til you sing it.*
> *Love in your heart wasn't put there to stay.*
> *Love isn't love 'til you give it away!*

Sandy exemplified sacrificial love. In 1998, after one year of marriage, Sandy's sister, Michele, was placed on the kidney donation list. She already had received kidney dialysis for the previous fifteen years. Dialysis works for a limited time before it becomes ineffective, and then the patient needs a do-nor kidney. Sandy called Michele and told her, "I am giving you my kidney." Michele resisted and stated they probably would not be a match, preferring to put herself on the donors list to obtain a stranger's kidney. Agreeing with Michele, I attempted to stop Sandy from donating her kidney since we had been recently married, and I didn't want a surgeon cutting her up or risking her life. Also, Michele was the third sibling in Sandy's family who had needed a kidney transplant, and Sandy would benefit from keeping her extra kidney. She responded, "I'm doing this, and you're going with me to support me." In conclusion, I could not argue against somebody saving another person's life. After the preliminary medical tests were done, Sandy was a six-out-of-seven match in the categories needed for kidney donation. Only an identical twin is a seven-out-of-seven match. A few months later, we flew halfway across the country to Michele's home. The hospital team performed a successful trans-plant. To this day, Michele has adopted the kidney almost as if it were her own. We have heard the saying, "He is so generous he would give the shirt off his own back." Well, Sandy did not question or hesitate giving her kidney from her own back to save the life of her sister.

True caregivers are called to love without counting the cost of their ac-tions. Some dementia literature states the term "caretaker" or "care-part-ner" as synonymous of "caregiver." I do not prefer to use the terms "care-taker" or "care-partner." They do not fully illuminate what the actions of a healthy person are toward the person with dementia. I can "take" care (caretaker) of someone, but if I "give" care (caregiver) to someone, it has a richer meaning. Additionally, as care-partner the meaning of having a "partnership" is one-sided. In the dynamics of the relationship between a healthy person and a person with dementia, there is no mutual exchange of love, which is the fullest definition of marriage. The healthy person is *giving* the care but not *receiving* any care from the other. Being a "care-giver" is a true act of love, giving unconditionally (agape love), without receiving or expecting anything in return. Those who are the least lovable are those who need the most love.

When Sandy's dementia became evident to the public, friends approached me, stating, "You're a saint." They complimented me on the strategies I used to deal with Sandy's irrational behaviors, my patience with her aggression, and my overall love for my spouse. Although humbled by their compliments, I have no feeling of merit. I am confident that if I displayed the same behaviors of this disease, Sandy would have unconditionally cared for me. Before the disease struck, she always tried to outdo me in thoughtfulness and charity. Being on stage as a caregiver, you need to rehearse your lines, have passion for your role, and be versatile in performing the various demands of the play.

Act III

The Search for a Diagnosis and Living with the Unknown

The term *dementia* can be misunderstood by the general population. Many people use the term Alzheimer's to explain someone with memory loss. Dementia has become the umbrella term for diseases of memory loss. The dementia umbrella includes the following:

- *Alzheimer's*—problems with memory, thinking, and behavior
- *Vascular dementia*—impairment from reduced blood flow to part of the brain
- *Mixed dementia*—Alzheimer's and one or more other dementias that occur together
- *Parkinson's disease*—dementia that develops in the late stages of this disease
- *Lewy body disease*—memory problems experienced with visual hallucinations, muscle rigidity, and tremors

- *Physical injury to the brain*—an accident or trauma that damages brain cells
- *Huntington's disease*—irregular movements of the limbs, changes in personality, and lack of thinking clearly
- *Creutzfeld-Jakob disease*—memory and behavior changes caused by eating meat affected by mad cow disease
- *Frontotempora*—impairment of the front and side areas of the brain, which affects personality and behavior changes
- *Normal pressure hydrocephalus*—buildup of fluid in the brain, which causes difficulty in walking, memory, and controlling urination
- *Mild cognitive impairment*—having memory problems that don't seriously affect one's daily life

("Basics of Alzheimer's Disease," *Alzheimer's Association,* 2012)

The area of the brain that is impaired reveals the different types of behaviors the patient exhibits. Each person with dementia has his or her own personality. Some of the behaviors and symptoms are similar to other patients, but no two patients are exactly alike in their traits, disposition, and temperament.

Dementia literature states this disease is broken down into seven progressive stages (normal outward behavior, very mild changes, mild decline, moderate decline, moderate severe decline, severe decline, and very severe decline). The life expectancy of a patient can be from a few years to a decade. In a small minority of cases, a person can live with dementia for more than twenty years.
(Barber Voss Home Care, *Information and Tips for Family Care Giving,* "Alzheimer's Care," 2015)

In 2009, the twelfth year of our marriage, I noticed the first stage of Sandy's dementia. When I came home from work, she started the conversation with "How was your day?" In a monologue lasting five or ten minutes, I shared the positive events of the day and vented about the negative stories. Sandy's sympathy helped me release my frustrations so that I could relieve stress and not bring it into the home. A few minutes later, she repeated, "So how was your day?"

In frustration, I replied, "I just told you."

She defensively responded, "I'm only trying to make conversation." During this time, my father was displaying the last stage of his Alzheimer's. I feared that I was at the beginning of the same play but with a different cast.

In the mornings, when Sandy looked up the day's schedule of her salon clients, she reviewed the appointments up to five times. By the third time, I knew the names, times, and procedures to be done, but she still did not know them. After I summarized the schedule of the day—"Bob for a haircut at 9:00 a.m., Mary for a perm at 11:00 a.m., and Sue for a manicure and pedicure at 1:00 p.m."—Sandy slammed her schedule book closed, denied any memory loss, and claimed she knew her business.

Knowing the stages of my father's dementia, I became concerned about Sandy's cognitive abilities. I decided to be proactive and made an appointment with our general practitioner. He performed a short memory test. After observing moderate memory loss, he set up a referral to the only neurologist who accepted our HMO insurance. I explained Sandy's symptoms to the neurologist. Sandy spoke about her accident in 1981. The doctor gave her the same memory test as our physician did and concluded that the MRI and CAT scan were negative for any malformations. He diagnosed her with mild cognitive impairment (MCI). I pondered, "Didn't I already know this? Isn't this similar to a patient who meets a doctor while coughing, and the doctor says, 'You have a cough.'"

The neurologist said that the cause of Sandy's dementia was brain damage from the car accident. I asked the doctor how he knew this. He replied, "Sandy told me."

In my silence and confusion, I asked myself, "Why is he taking the past memories as historical facts from a dementia patient?"

While I was still feeling confused and perplexed about the diagnosis, the doctor confidently summarized his prognosis by saying, "Please make an appointment in three months for a follow-up."

When we returned three months later, I encouraged the neurologist to read my journal in private concerning Sandy's past behaviors. It stated, "Sandy is taking valuable items that do not belong to her," and, "She did not know what state we were in while traveling last week." While staying at my mother's house in Las Vegas, Sandy took my mom's small antique dolls out of the cabinet and placed them in her suitcase; when caught, she claimed that my father gave her permission to have these (but at this time, he was in the memory clinic). Sandy also took a hundred-dollar bottle of perfume from my sister's bathroom and put it in her purse. When we flew from Las Vegas, Nevada, to visit my sister in Phoenix, Arizona, Sandy thought we were still in Las Vegas.

After reading my notes, the neurologist asked Sandy, "Is it true that you were stealing and that you did not know what state you were in while on vacation last week?" Obviously, she denied both accusations, as denial is normal in this disease. The only benefit of this neurologist was the ability to prescribe medications for agitation.

The medication claimed to slow down the progression of disease, but I believe there is no proof that it is effective. No one can clone another Sandy to determine the difference between the one taking the medication and the other not taking it. At times, I wondered if memory medications are a placebo for the caregiver so that we feel something is being done for our loved one.

In the early stages of Sandy's disease, we started to attend sessions at the memory center at Methodist Hospital. On staff is a neuropsychologist who conducts testing to determine the baselines of the ability to retain and process information and to mark its progression. The tests concluded that Sandy's diagnosis was frontotemporal dementia, displayed by disability in rational thought, planning events, and short-term memory loss. To me, this diagnosis seemed reasonable and at least more definitive than the neurologist's was. Sandy's traits did not follow the normal pattern of Alzheimer's as I had witnessed with my father; she was too young to be forgetful, and her first signs were difficulties in making plans in the business and in organizing her daily life. It seemed logical that the accident and other past head traumas had affected the frontal and temporal lobes of the brain. We attended sessions every six months to measure the disease's progression. Our neurologist received the reports from the neuropsychologist but claimed that he did not believe in the conclusion.

Hoping to get a definitive answer regarding the diagnosis, I requested a PET scan on Sandy's brain from our primary doctor. These show more detailed mapping than MRI and CAT scans do. Our doctor told me that this procedure is too expensive and unnecessary because in dementia, one knows the diagnosis of the patient by the symptoms. When I stated that I wanted to have empirical evidence of Sandy's disability, he replied, "You need to get over this empirical thing."

In July 2014, during the moderate stages of Sandy's dementia, I attended a meeting with the Frontotemporal Association. They were in the planning stages to start a new chapter in our area. Fortunately, before the lecture began, I was privileged to partake in a private conversation with the neuropsychiatrist. As a professor at the local prestigious medical school, she had the expertise to present the lecture on dementia and frontotemporal dementia. After explaining Sandy's history and behaviors, the professor suggested a possible diagnosis of post-concussion syndrome. This occurs when a person who has had numerous concussions, such as athletes who play football or box, develops deterioration of brain functioning earlier than the general population. The professor's analysis was enlightening and reasonable, but now the stage was getting crowded with too many possible diagnoses.

I diligently researched Sandy's running accident to know the validity, cause, severity, and treatment. When I contacted Sandy's current friends, none of them knew her in 1981. Speaking with her three children, they said that during that year, all of them were less than five years old, and all they remembered was their mom being in the hospital for a long time. When I conversed with her siblings, none of them said they visited her at the hospital. They only received information and updates from her former husband, who was very unreliable. I called the medical records departments at the four local hospitals nearest Sandy's home, but they all have policies that their medical records are expunged after seven years. A few months ago, when her youngest son, Peter, asked his father what really happened in the accident, the story was rewritten. His dad told Peter that while Sandy was driving a car and going to a destination she should not have been going (claiming Sandy was having an affair), she ended up being hit by another car. After this tale, which Peter had never heard previously, I wondered if the "accident" was actually an abusive incident by the ex-husband. By this point, I gave up on knowing the truth of the background of Sandy's head trauma. I needed to resign myself to deal only with the present and the future.

During the most recent session with Sandy's neurologist and having the latest information about her disease, I asked for an exact diagnosis. "Dementia/Alzheimer's, something like that," he replied. With all of the doctor's training and knowledge, I was stunned that the vague diagnosis continued. In truth, an accurate diagnosis that all agree on may not be discovered. Desiring to understand or at least have a label for what was happening to my wife, I needed to grasp that ultimately obtaining a diagnosis was insignificant since dementia cannot be cured but only managed by behavioral interventions.

In the beginning stages of dementia, Sandy became obsessive in her toileting behaviors. If idle, she felt compelled to use the bathroom every few minutes, even if she had very little to urinate, and nobody could talk her out of it. When I came home from work, I daily discovered three or four rolls of toilet paper tubes in the trash can. She used five- to ten-foot strips at one sitting, even in public toilets. During my father's wake, while I greeted the guests, Sandy backed up all of the toilets at the funeral home. I sarcastically informed my family that if they wanted to buy me a valued Christmas present, send me cases of toilet paper. The excessive flushing of the toilet actually doubled the water bill in our home.

Every few months, Sandy adopted a new obsession:
- turning off the furnace in the middle of winter
- continually starting the dishwasher after the dishes were clean
- wearing the same clothes every day
- lighting candles and incense around the house
- decorating the house in a sloppy manner
- closing all of the curtains during the day and turning all of the lights on
- putting every item that was placed on the counters away (in places I may never find)
- chopping off the vegetables and fruits before they were ripe and cutting all of the flowers in our garden
- turning off the answering machine
- calling my cell phone every few minutes, starting at exactly 6:00 p.m., to see when I was coming home
- having an inner drive to leave wherever she was
- placing unnecessary items in the shopping cart while she was pushing it

To counteract these odd behaviors, I became proficient in managing our household using the following techniques:
- taping the thermostat shut
- emptying the dishwasher immediately after finishing
- after she fell asleep, washing her outfit and putting a new outfit on the same hanger
- throwing away the candles and incense

- determining which lights in the house were unnecessary and hiding those light bulbs
- hiding the garden shears, hammer, and nails
- immediately placing the mail, bills, food, pens, glasses, keys, cell phone (or any other item I would need later) in their proper area
- setting one roll of toilet paper on a shelf, out of reach, and personally distributing pieces of toilet paper to her
- turning off my cell phone at 6:05 p.m. (even though she filled the voicemail with twenty messages)
- making sure the answering machine remained on
- finding ways to keep her stationary (e.g., favorite TV shows, avoidance of busy public areas, giving her personal attention)
- always standing next to the shopping cart in order to put the items back

To my surprise, I discovered an organization, Memory Care Home Solutions, which assists in finding household items and creating strategies to help caregivers navigate the new and strange behaviors they face. Dealing with a dementia patient is analogous to sitting in the orchestra pit and learning to play a new instrument every few months.

Act IV

Facing the Tragedy

When Sandy was officially diagnosed with dementia, she was sixty-one years old, and I was fifty-one. Five million people in this country are diagnosed with dementia, and only two hundred thousand are under age sixty-five, according to the Alzheimer's Association. While seeking and locating a local Alzheimer's support group, I began to process my array of emotions: feeling the grief and loss of my father, who was in the last stages of Alzheimer's, and mostly the frustration of being surprised and too young and unwilling to be dealing with my wife in the first stages of dementia. I felt doomed at the thought of going through the journey of watching a loved one fade away again.

Noticing that others in the support group were either spouses in their eighties facing the losses of their loved ones (to whom they had been married for fifty-plus years) or daughters caring for their elderly parents, my thoughts were, "I'm a middle-aged man and married only fifteen years. The others in the group are dealing with loved ones who have already lived a full life and are at the end of their lives anyway. I'm supposed to be at the prime of my life, and now I have no hope!"

When it was my turn to talk, I spoke about how well my mother was caring for my father and that recently my wife had been diagnosed with dementia. "My life sucks!" I whined to the group and questioned why this was happening to me. I sarcastically asked, "Was God stating that since I've been experiencing my father's Alzheimer's for the past six years, I am an expert and can be proficient in dealing with my wife?" I dreaded to live out the motto "practice makes perfect." Don't we know the sequel is never as good as the original?

After my bitter monologue, one of the facilitators of the support group, being in awe and sympathy of my situation, said to me, "You should write a book."

Bitterness toward my new situation and my lack of concern for the others in the support group were obvious. After the meeting, the other facilitator, a trained counselor, spoke privately with me and recommended that I attend individual sessions with her. She noticed that I tended to come across as unsupportive in the support group. Being directed to attend individual counseling was the best advice I received in all of the years of managing Sandy's diagnosis. No one can carry the cross alone. For more than two years, I have been attending individual sessions every three to four weeks. These give me the knowledge, wisdom, and courage to carry on. The best players on the stage are those who learn and grow into their parts from the cues of a qualified director.

In 2012, my mother needed to admit my father into a memory clinic. After his admission, Sandy and I visited my parents and toured my father's memory-care facility. Sandy was in the mild stages of decline, and I sarcastically whispered in my mother's ear, "Are you sure that Dad doesn't need a roommate?" My mother, being in her late seventies, put her health at risk in caring for my father at home. My parents had the house to themselves, and Mom constantly needed to supervise and attend to my father's hygiene, whereabouts, and tantrums. In the late stages, Dad was getting out of bed numerous times during the night and trying to walk out of the house; my mother would stop him but lost a lot of sleep. One time, while my mother was sitting in the beauty-salon chair, my father left the salon and attempted to walk home. He wanted to leave and did not tell her. He fell and hit his head, and a stranger found Dad. The police transported him to the hospital and found my mother's contact information in my father's wallet.

My dad's anger erupted unprovoked, and a few times, he yelled and cocked back his fist as if to hit my mother. Her anxiety wore her down as she watched her husband fade away. My father, who played eighteen holes of golf almost daily during his retirement, was reduced to putting on the living-room carpet; he used to read novels, biographies, and educational books, but he had deteriorated to simply watching TV. At least this hobby remained constant.

While Sandy's condition continued to deteriorate, I tried to keep my life as normal as possible, continuing with my work and social life while not admitting to anyone the difficulties in my marriage, my emotional stress, and Sandy's diagnosis. One morning, while on the road driving to work, I encountered our new associate pastor, Father Andrew. Stopping at the same red light and rolling down our windows, he yelled, "At what hospital is your stepson, Peter?" I became frightened and perplexed because I knew nothing about a medical emergency with Peter. Yelling back, I told Father Andrew to pull over to a side street. He informed me that yesterday he greeted my wife in the church parking lot. She told him that she was headed to the chapel to pray for her son who was in a car accident. Later on that day, Father Andrew visited the two hospitals in our area and could not locate Peter's name on the registry.

Pausing and realizing there was no accident, I needed to let the truth come out about Sandy's condition. I told Father Andrew that Peter was fine. He was home this morning and not in the hospital. Then I informed him of Sandy's diagnoses and the condition of "con-fabrication"—a condition in which dementia patients make up stories to fill in the blanks in their minds in order to appear coherent. Father Andrew became the first person outside of my immediate family to hear about Sandy's dementia. He compassionately understood my situation and was glad to hear that Peter was fine. I felt relieved at finally telling someone outside of my family about my problem, but I was also saddened and embarrassed by the fact that Sandy's bizarre behavior had been exposed to outsiders.

Act V

Acting Out from Frustration

As the disease progressed in 2013 and 2014, Sandy's behavior became more impulsive, angrier, and more aggressive. In the first agitation incident, Sandy accused me of throwing away her wine that was in the refrigerator from the previous day. Waking me up early in the morning from a deep sleep, she yelled at me for being such a cruel and horrible husband because I either drank or poured her wine down the sink. She didn't remember that she had finished the bottle herself the previous day. Sandy knew that I never drink alcohol. It creates an upset stomach; besides this, she had no justification in believing I would want to pour out her wine.

The incidents of aggression increased. Whenever I disagreed with her, she would call me "liar," "fat," and "lazy." She forgot that I'm an honest man, only 150 pounds, and I work forty-five to fifty hours per week. During her tantrums, my name was not Tom; my new name was too vulgar to mention. Whenever I corrected or guided her, even in minor matters—such as, "It's time to brush your teeth"—I heard back, "Shut up, not listening," or, "You only think of yourself." Getting ready to go to bed, we prepared ourselves in the bathroom together. When she left the bathroom with me walking behind her, she would turn off the light and close the door in my face. If her angry moments occurred when exiting the car, she would slam the car door as hard as possible. One time her anger erupted when I stated it was unnecessary to put the leash on our dog when the dog was on the couch in my lap. She took our tiny old dog from me, threw the dog onto the other couch next to me, and then stomped off.

Her anger flared up mostly in the mornings. One of the behaviors that people with dementia display is called "sundowning." It describes patients who get angry and anxious at the end of the day due to fatigue. They can pace, scream, and be physically aggressive. I called Sandy's ailment "sun rising": the difficulty of adjusting to a new day. The anger arose as soon as she awakened and without any provocation. In the morning, if I said hello, to our dog, she sassed back, "Shut up, this is my dog." Due to her "sun rising" I learned that while getting ready for work, I needed not to say anything, quickly shower, get dressed, and head out the door, eating breakfast in the car in order to depart faster. There are two ways to greet the morning: one can say, "Good morning, God," or one can say, "Good God, it's morning!" Sandy did the latter.

Sandy also developed separation anxiety when I left her range of sight—while we were together in our house, when I left for work in the morning, or when I left for meetings in the evening. Never admitting it, Sandy became more dependent on me for keeping her on track throughout the day. In the house, she followed me wherever I went—using the toilet, cleaning the house, doing yard work, cooking, and so forth. Experts call this "shadowing." In the morning, wearing pajamas and with a purse on her shoulder, she emphatically claimed, "I am coming with you." After I politely and gently stated that I needed to go to work, her response was unapologetic, and she proceeded to enter the garage with me. Rarely, she consented to stay inside. When I pursed my lips attempting a good-bye kiss, she would turn her face to the side because she was upset with me. I ended up kissing her on the cheek. While backing the car out, I would regularly be cursed out. One time while I was backing out, she kicked the front fender of my car. Since Sandy took sign-language classes, we had a tradition when I pulled out of the driveway. We would always exchange the "I love you" sign (a closed hand with the index and pinky finger up); now with Sandy being easily irritated, she responded to me with her own sign (her middle finger raised high in the air).

Trauma at home meant work became my respite and oasis. It gave me the chance to converse with my coworkers, who were good listeners, kind, and rational, and who remembered and understood whatever I told them. What an irony! In my career as a social worker (case manager in foster care for twenty-one years), I was frequently attacked by my clients, and I was not affected by them. I engaged parents of neglected or abused children and children diagnosed with behavior disorders. These parents and children had issues of mental health, substance abuse, sexual abuse (victims and perpetrators), domestic violence, anger management, poor bonding and trust, limited intellect, and so forth. Parents tend to hate caseworkers because their children have been removed from their care, and children tend to be angry because they are away from their home. Emotionally, I'm able to manage verbal abuse or anger from those with whom I have a worker-client relationship, but from a spouse, these attacks pierced through my heart. It was very difficult not to take these attacks personally and to understand that it did not come from Sandy but from the disease.

Behavior-management techniques were ineffective with Sandy and are not successful for most people with dementia. A behavior plan requires the recipient to have some reasoning ability and forethought to understand a plan, agree with the plan, and carry it out. Healthy children and even behavior-disordered children eventually learn to avoid a behavior because they do not want a negative consequence. A dementia patient lacks the cognitive ability to know the cause and effect of his or her behaviors, and he or she does not remember what he or she did or what will be the consequences. Therefore, no contingency plan is helpful. Her son Peter nicknamed Sandy "ten-second Sandy." This literally was how long she could remember an action or a statement. Since behavior-management techniques to curb the agitation were not effective, we needed to pursue psychotropic medication. The neurologist prescribed fifty milligrams of Seroquel in the morning and the evening. This moderately assisted in calming down her moods.

The violent scenes of this play were the most difficult and challenging to watch and address. I got through this act only by the grace of God and the support from others. During this phase of managing Sandy's dementia, my only consolation in being with her was that at least I was not alone in our house.

INTERMISSION

Occasional Relief

Most days my only relief was when Sandy would fall asleep first. Although the dementia play is long, and one suffers watching it and playing his or her role, at times one can cherish his or her spouse's love. Sandy showed glimpses of her "old self" when she laughed at my jokes, took my hand to walk through our garden, and complimented me on my cooking, cleaning, or gardening, stating, "You're my husband and a good man." These moments became more valuable than they were before her dementia. I seized these moments and felt grateful.

Now back to the show.

Act VI

Experiencing Shock, Awe, and Disgust

From 2012 to 2014, Sandy, who took pride as a business owner, progressively lost clients from her hair- and skin-care business due to her lack of organizational skills and poor quality of work. Sandy earned a total yearly salary of $700 in 2013 and nothing in 2014. A client and twenty-year friend showed me her lopsided haircut and spoke about the perm chemicals being left on her hair past the allotted time. For seventeen years, I had sarcastically stated, "I married Sandy in order to get a lifetime of free haircuts." Sandy's decline forced me to locate a stylist at a local chain salon. This transition away from Sandy to an unknown salon was more difficult than I imagined, and I experienced grieving for another loss in our relationship.

Sandy placed the business bill statements in her purse. Carrying these reminded her to drive to the bank, obtain cashier's checks, and pay the balance. In the summer of 2013, I noticed two AT&T bills for the business phone in her purse. She promised me that once she finished a "high-roller" client who was coming in this week, she would pay the bill. A few weeks later, I discovered a third AT&T bill in her purse. It still was not paid. At this time, I took

24

control of the situation, and she was furious. I paid the bills myself, cancelled the business phone number, and forwarded the clients' calls to our home line. I knew the business was disintegrating because Sandy could no longer manage her schedule or finances (e.g., when a client called to schedule an appointment, Sandy opened her scheduling book and wrote down the appointment on the first page she saw). For the next two months, she reminded me how mean I was because I cut off her business phone. About a month later, she lost touch with what had happened, and she never mentioned it again.

In May 2013, Sandy started to fill her day with driving to the bank, picking up the mail from the PO box, and then driving home. A short time later, she repeated this cycle and continued it throughout the day. In one month, she made seventy bank transactions, sometimes making seven to eight in one day: withdrawing ten dollars, depositing five dollars, withdrawing six dollars, depositing five dollars, and so on. This money was spent on gas and items she did not need at the discount stores (pictures, statues, extra purses, etc.). Within two months, she drained her three accounts and was no longer able to contribute financially to the family. I discovered this obsessive behavior a month after it occurred while organizing her bank receipts for the preparation of taxes. The staff at Sandy's bank was restricted from speaking to me about this issue due to the confidentiality of her accounts. After all of Sandy's accounts were closed, I spoke with the bank manager and tellers. When I explained her dementia, they were relieved because they did not understand the reason for the obsessive withdrawals and deposits.

In June 2013, during Sandy's constant driving from home, to the bank, and to the post office, she ran out of gas in our neighborhood. Peter needed to push her car down the street and into the garage. A few minutes later, Sandy left the house to do her obsessive routine and started the car. She backed the car out of the garage. On the driveway, the car ran out of gas again, and Peter pushed it back into the garage. Thirty minutes later, Sandy tried to start the car, but it would not start. The next day, I consulted with my support counselor about the incident and my plan of action. Driving was the only duty that gave Sandy purpose in those days. When I came home from work, she was proud to show me the mail she had obtained. However, my counselor explained that if Sandy could not read the sign of being out of gas, then she might not be able to navigate all that happens when driving. That night, when Sandy fell asleep, I took her car keys out of her purse and hid them.

The next day, when she questioned where her keys were, I bluntly stated, "I don't know, and besides, there's no gas in the car anyway." This was a very difficult decision. Driving is a normal part of being a responsible adult, and I needed to admit to myself that Sandy was not a responsible adult anymore. For about one month, when I told Sandy, "I don't know where the car keys are," she bitterly said I was lying. (Actually, this time I was.) About a month later, she forgot about not having the keys, and she did not mention it again. As a caregiver, we need to be confident that there is no such thing as "lying" when dealing with dementia patients; it's simply making up stories to keep them safe.

To confirm the right decision was made in removing her driving privileges, I arranged a driving exam at our local rehab hospital. The driving coach informed me that they would be away for the driving exam for forty-five to sixty minutes. After only twenty minutes, they came back. He announced that Sandy had committed four driving offenses: running a stop sign in the parking lot, making a left into oncoming traffic, being too close to another car when parking, and not staying in the lines on the road. He recommended that it was not safe for Sandy to drive anymore. Sandy's response was calm but defiant, stating that she had taught all of her sons to drive. With this exam, I confirmed that I had made the right decision. Similar to any medical decision, it's always good to get a second opinion.

By the winter of 2014, Sandy ceased performing personal hygiene and self-care. Being in the cosmetology business and always needing to look her best for her clients, she had been diligent about her appearance, even to the point of being late for social outings and appointments. The preparation to obtain the beauty she desired took at least an hour. One time when my mother was visiting us, my wife was late getting ready to go out for dinner. My mother yelled up the stairs, "Let's go; you're not going to the prom!"

Sandy did not bathe for months. I was at a loss on how to get her into the shower. When I requested she take a shower, she would say that she took one already this morning or that she would do it later. One time I bribed her with ten dollars. Sandy did not believe that I would pay, so I gave her the money beforehand. She took the ten-dollar bill, went into the walk-in closet, put it in her purse, and then came back out. I boasted, "Now you can take a shower since I gave you the money."

She questioned, "What money?"

At this point, I said to myself, "I give up!" An expert in the field of dementia stated that it's very common for those with dementia to not like water; to them it feels like needles hitting them. Sandy's hair, which was once a bright, shiny blond, became a flat, greasy, pewter color. Her nails, which had always been perfectly manicured, became uneven with chipped polish. Her clothes, formerly classy and stylish, didn't match. She wore the same outfit every day.

In May 2014, one hot and humid Saturday, Sandy assisted me in the backyard, repairing an outside fence. At the end of the chore, I asked if she was going to take a shower. She responded with a definitive yes. I knew her response was merely words. My frustration boiled over, so I took the garden hose and sprayed her down. Sandy became angry, knocked over the trashcan full of yard waste, and screamed that she was going to divorce me and call the police. I was hoping the neighbors didn't hear this. Then she ran inside with me following her, and she yelled at me, stating, "Now I have to take a shower," which she did. In thanking God for the miracle, relief and joy consumed me as I had the opportunity to prepare the shower for her. It's not recommended to use violent means to get the end one desires. In fact, I never did it again. It came out of desperation and frustration and the fact that I did not want to smell her odor.

One Saturday morning in May one week later, a worker from a lawn treatment and fertilizing company rang our doorbell. I thought he was soliciting business, but he informed me that he was ready to start the treatments on our lawn today. It consisted of four weeks of treatment at a cost of $300. I asked if he had the correct address. He confirmed the address and showed me the work order. I told him that I never ordered it. In fact, my grass was already green and didn't need it. I thought it was a scam, but he said that he received the order from the corporate office and showed me the statement. He left our home, and I proceeded to call the manager of the business. The manager said that they called our home last week advertising their company, and a woman answered the phone and accepted their services. Now the lights came on. I told her that my wife has dementia. They apologized and cancelled the order. Fortunately, that Saturday morning I was home. If not, who else could have taken advantage of Sandy, and how much could this have cost?

In June 2014, Sandy started to walk from our house and go into the neighbors' homes without knocking. She told the neighbors that she was locked out of her house or lost her dog and wondered if it was in their home. One evening, when Peter was home with his mother, without his knowing, Sandy walked across the street into the new neighbor's house and said she wanted to go to church with them. Fortunately, the young husband was a Baptist minister and his mother-in-law, who was visiting, knew the signs of dementia because she dealt with her aunt who was diagnosed with it. They sent Sandy home and explained to Peter what happened.

In July 2014, while I was an hour away from home driving a six-year-old foster child to a visit with her father, I received a call from Peter, who was also at work an hour away from home. He said that he received a call from the police that Sandy refused to leave the house across the street. The construction worker was using a sledgehammer to knock down walls inside of the house. Sandy quietly entered the house, and she was almost hit. When she was commanded to leave the house, being overly curious, she returned three more times. This led the construction worker to call the police, who ordered her to go home. Since I was an hour away from home, I phoned a friend who lived a few blocks from my house. This friend was a former police officer and was willing to speak to the police and watch Sandy until I came home. When I arrived, I noticed a ticket on the refrigerator door stating that Sandy had committed trespassing. No charges were filed.

January 2, 2015 (an *un*happy new year), a date that will forever be etched into my mind, I showered and dressed while Sandy was sleeping. I woke her so that she could get ready for our dental appointment. She went into the walk-in closet to get dressed and shut the door. Immediately, a roar of frustration came out of the closet. When I opened the door, Sandy was lying on the floor, curled up in a fetal position, drooling and shaking. She was having a grand mal seizure. Frantically, I dialed 911, and the police and the ambulance came quickly and took her to the local hospital. Fortunately, the MRI was negative for stroke. Sandy fractured her pelvis by falling on the hardwood floor, and she was unable to walk due to the pain. After one week of hospitalization, Sandy was placed in a rehab nursing home for physical therapy for two weeks. After the rehab, Sandy needed to be admitted to a long-term-care nursing home due to nobody being able to supervise her at home full-time. The only care available was paid home care through an agency. These home-care agencies are great assets, but they charge an average of nineteen dollars per hour; I was at work forty hours per week, which equals $39,520 per year for care, which was my take-home salary. Therefore, I was cornered into placing Sandy in a long-term-care nursing home.

For seventeen years, I had slept with Sandy every night. She was my constant companion in our social events, daily chores, errands, and recreational activities. During our marriage, I was only away from Sandy on two weekends for business trips. It was terribly lonely without her. I looked forward to visiting her during evenings for dinner and bringing her home on the weekends.

During the two weeks Sandy was rehabbing in the initial nursing home, I investigated the long-term-care nursing homes that were designated as "Medicaid pending" and that accepted dementia patients. Speaking with friends who worked in the nursing-home field, we reviewed the types and reputations of various homes in the area. Other aids were websites that critiqued nursing homes. By consulting my elder-care attorney, we determined who could assist with the Medicaid application, either the lawyer or the nursing-home staff. Numerous phone calls to various nursing homes and discussions with several heads of admissions helped me to determine if Sandy was a correct match. The search narrowed down to meeting the staff and touring three nursing homes.

Favoring one of the homes ten miles from my house, I started working with the business manager on the forms for Medicaid. This nursing home had to do a procedural interview with Sandy before admission. They interviewed her the day before she needed to be released from the temporary rehab nursing home because my insurance company had denied extending her stay. The admission officer informed me that the interview had only lasted a few minutes because Sandy responded to his statements with "I am going to chop off your head and kill you." Therefore, this facility denied her admission.

My thoughts were "What did you ask her because she doesn't say this to strangers?" and "Don't memory clinics deal with volatile clients daily?" Now I was the one who was so disappointed and angry that I wanted to chop his head off and kill him. After this, I was at a loss. I had twenty-four hours to find a facility, or she would be homeless. Sandy was not able to come home because we had steps in our house, and I could not care for her when I was at work.

Sandy always had a devotion to Saint Joseph, husband of Mary and foster father of Jesus. She admired how a man who was unrelated to Jesus and who discovered his betrothed was pregnant would unconditionally care for both of them. This is noted as background for the next scene of the play.

Fortunately, within the twenty-four hours before Sandy needed to be discharged, the initial rehab/nursing home contacted another nursing home in our area that I did not know or investigate. This other nursing home was

Medicaid pending, and they took dementia patients unconditionally. In fear I thought, "What about the interview?" Fortunately, that same day, they completed the interview, and Sandy was nonthreatening. Then I worried that I never investigated or visited this home. Well, at this point, being desperate and out of time, I could not be anxious about this placement. The day my insurance company ceased payment to the initial rehab/nursing home was the day Sandy was admitted to the long-term-care nursing home. When I looked on the map to locate the facility, I was surprised by what building sat next door, no more than fifty yards away. The name of the building? Saint Joseph Church. A sign and lesson learned: resign oneself, because no matter how hard one tries to control one's life, God is still in control.

Act VII

Laughter Is the Best Medicine

One of the comforts during these trying times was being with "man's best friend," our dog of fifteen years. Even though our dog is old, she still desires to sleep in my bed and lies next to me while I watch TV. In the past year, our dog suffered from a skin infection in which she lost about half of her hair follicles. She also started to go potty in the house. My vet said that this was due to "canine senility." In the past few months, Sandy needed to wear adult diapers, especially at night. Also, Sandy's hairstylist said that her hair was thinning, possibly due to her medication. One needs to laugh at the similarities. Why was it that those I loved and lived in my house had dementia, were losing their hair, and were becoming incontinent?

As Sandy's disease progressed into the moderate/late stages, she became more simple, concrete, and childlike. For her, there was no past or future; she lived only in the present. Humorously, Sandy was the five-year-old daughter I never had. I learned greater tolerance and enjoyment by being in her presence as one has in being with a child. There's a saying in the dementia world about being able to care and manage them: "The worse they get, the better they get."

Although this also involved the grieving that Sandy, the way I knew her, was fading away, the lesson learned was that "if you don't laugh, you'll cry." This loss of a loved one is a long-term process of grieving that is never fully completed. I used to say that Sandy was only 10 percent of herself; the other 90 percent was a strange foreigner whom I hated. As time goes on, I'm slowly embracing the idea of acceptance, which was aided by Sandy's developing a childlike sense of humor. Following are a collection of Sandy's humorous sayings or stories that kept me enjoying her presence:

"Did you hear that Amtrak just went mobile?"

"Sir, you wrote down the wrong date of my birthday; that's the birthday of my twin sister."

I called Sandy and said, "Hello. What are you doing now?"
She responded, "Answering the phone and talking to you."

It was 8:00 p.m. and the grandfather clock rang eight times. Sandy said, "See, the clock keeps perfect time."

A friend stated to Sandy, "You're having your nails grow out long." Sandy responded, "No, the nails are growing themselves."

After I observed our dog's behavior, I said, "I think the dog is sick."
Sandy said, "No the dog is fine."
So I said, "But the dog is acting lethargic."
Sandy replied, "The dog is not acting."

I said, "We need to vacuum this carpet."
Sandy replied, "It can't be done; there is only one vacuum." (Notice the pronoun "we.")

I waved to the clerk at the grocery store.

Sandy asked, "Who are you waving to?"
I replied, "Mimi."
Sandy said, "How can you say hi to yourself?"

I have rosacea, so when it flares up, my cheeks and nose get red. One Sunday, near the end of service, we went up to the altar and received Holy Communion. After we received Our Lord in communion, we went back to the pew to pray intimately with Jesus. Sandy immediately turned to me and asked me why my face was so red. I said, in a tone of not wanting to make a conversation, "I'm praying."
So she replied, "Well, quit trying so hard."

Sandy and I were sitting on the couch together watching TV. An ad came on about ChristianMingle.com. The commercial showed a testimony from a couple who fell in love after meeting on the website. They stated, "As Christians we get together as a couple to make each other better." So I asked Sandy, "Do I make you better?"
She replied in her simple way, "No, I'm good."

I asked her, "Why are you wearing three watches on one wrist?"
Sandy replied, "One for each time zone."
At another time she replied, "This way I don't run out of time."

When we were at any dinner table, Sandy always took the paper napkins and paper tubes from the straws, twisted them, and tied them in a knot. I asked Sandy, "Why do you always put the napkins and paper in a knot?"
She replied, "So they don't untie."

I told Sandy that tomorrow was our wedding anniversary, and she could pick out any fancy restaurant for dinner. "Where do you want to go?"

She replied, "McDonald's."

SUPPORTING CAST

The "No Shows" and the Award Winners

When following the plot of the dementia play became more difficult, I sought out friends and family for support, hoping they could spend time with Sandy while I was at work by giving her companionship, keeping her mind active, and stopping her from wandering away from the house. Similar to raising a child, it takes a village to support the caregiver and the one with dementia.

One of Sandy's friends of twenty-plus years, Nina, said she would be more than happy to help. She loved Sandy. When Nina called the day before to confirm her first outing, Sandy hung up the phone, thinking it was a telemarketer. When Nina called back, I explained what had happened, and then we confirmed a lunch outing for noon the following day. Twelve o'clock passed, and Nina came an hour later. The second social date, Nina came late again. Afterward, Nina informed me that her tardiness was caused by having a panic attack prior to leaving the house. Hoping to reduce her stress, I asked her to learn about the disease of dementia and to give time for Sandy to adjust to a new routine. Nina called me back a few weeks later and informed me that her psychiatrist told her not to be involved with Sandy anymore.

Sandy enjoyed another twenty-plus-year friendship with Harriet, who stated she would be on stage with me during these difficult times. When Harriet's husband suddenly passed away seven years ago, Sandy had accompanied her daily, comforting her, taking her shopping, and being a companion. Since she lived alone and had appreciated Sandy's help in the past, I thought Harriet would naturally reciprocate. When asked if I could drop Sandy off at her house one or two days per week when I went to work, Harriet desired to know, "If I get impatient with her, will you be here to pick her up?" Therefore, I stopped seeking help from Harriet, and at this point, Sandy socialized with Harriet only when I was also present.

After this incident, I arranged plans to go out to lunch with Harriet and her sister who visits every year from Europe. I left a few messages for Harriet to set up the date, but Harriet procrastinated in returning my call. By the time I reached Harriet, she said that her sister left on the plane the previous day.

Suspicious, I confronted Harriet, asking if the reason why there was no lunch date set up was because of Sandy's dementia. Harriet said that it was true. Harriet's sister wanted to "remember Sandy the way she was." Was being with Sandy that uncomfortable? Dementia is not a contagious disease. One can remember how somebody was and, at the same time, know how somebody is.

One of the greatest disappointments in lacking help from friends or family concerned Sandy's sister, Michele. Having received Sandy's kidney, she was enjoying her new life free from the dialysis machine. In May 2013, I asked Michele for support, knowing that the disease would only become more difficult to manage by myself. Michele shrugged her shoulders, saying, "I need to finish my final year of employment before retirement and then spend time with my three grandchildren." Around this same time, Michele stopped calling Sandy. Michele said that she didn't know what to say to someone with dementia and that Sandy did not want to have extended conversations.

Sandy still remembered—and with much affection—her sister Michele. This loss of her sister's relationship and the neglect of receiving any help left a bitter taste with me that is difficult to forgive. Michele would not be alive if it weren't for Sandy's generosity, and when I needed support, she held the stance of being too busy and uncomfortable. In my frustration, I was tempted to say to Michele, "Well then, can you give back Sandy's kidney?"

Lacking the support of our family and local friends while Sandy was living with me, I turned to an in-home health-care company. The case manager came to our home for the interview. I explained the need for assistance in the home for Sandy. Peter worked full-time and was camping, and I worked more than forty hours per week. After the interview, we filled out the forms to begin services. The next day, the case manager called me and said that she had good news and bad news. The good news was that services were approved for twelve hours per week and that Medicaid could pay for it. The bad news was that she made a hot line call on me for neglecting my spouse, stating that she was a mandated reporter, and I was not permitted to leave my wife home alone. She told me that an elder-abuse investigator would be coming to my house unannounced.

I responded by saying that I had reached out my hand to her for assistance and she just bit it. My anger kindled as I explained my profession as a foster-care caseworker for twenty years, and part of my job was hot lining parents who abused and neglected their children. Emphatically, I said the elder-care investigation was not warranted. I had been searching out services for my wife for the past six months. This incident was a low point for me in managing dementia, especially because I needed to justify how I was caring for my wife. To make the wound worse, at work I needed to inform my direct supervisor, then the director of the program, and then the vice president of the agency about the hot line. They could have received a call from the investigator. Fortunately, after the investigator came to our house for the second time, he assessed that I knew how to manage Sandy, and he planned on dropping the case. Later on, I discovered it's rare for a case to be dropped so quickly. Watch out for social workers who are overeager to do their job.

A few months earlier, I had visited the local department of aging and discovered that they have a program called Senior Companions. They are elder volunteers who come to the house and care for your loved ones. Our names were on the waiting list for six months before I received a call stating that they had a woman, named Beth, who had been doing this work for years, and she was a good match for Sandy. The first session was an orientation meeting, and plans were made to start their companionship the following Monday. Beth said that she could care for Sandy 10:00 a.m. to 2:00 p.m., Monday through Thursday. I was very grateful; not only was it free, but I could go to work knowing that Sandy was safe with her new friend. On Thursday of the first week, Beth called me and confirmed Monday's appointment. The next day, Friday, the director of the program revealed that Beth did not want to be a companion with Sandy anymore and wanted to back out. Beth claimed that it was too difficult to make conversation with Sandy. Also, she did not know how to respond when Sandy told her to use the bathroom in Peter's bedroom while he was sleeping. The director said that they would still be looking for another provider. Since that time, the phone has been silent.

Peter and I brainstormed on who could be a caregiver for Sandy when I went to work. He had the idea that we could offer Sandy's oldest son, Sam, payment for staying in the house and caring for his mother. While thinking this was helpful financially for Sam, we were also hoping this could heal his relationship with her. For fifteen years, Sam had been claiming that their strained relationship was caused by his parents' divorce that occurred in his early twenties. Also, he believed that Sandy was abusive, giving him a horrible childhood. Sam stated that these traumas made his life problematic (e.g., difficulty maintaining employment, two marriages ending in divorce, having five children by three women, and surrendering his parental rights to his two older children). Sam had avoided contact with his mother for the past fifteen years but kept regular contact with his father. Informing Sam about Sandy's dementia and the need for twenty-four-hour care, his response was, "What a shame. Now Mom won't be able to understand how angry I am with her if I talk to her." Therefore, Peter and I quickly dropped the idea of Sam ever being supportive.

After trial and error, help came for Sandy from our local church. One great asset came from the Knights of Columbus brothers (a fraternal, charitable organization) and their wives. They showed me compassion, and they were not repulsed by Sandy's odd behaviors. Every Saturday evening, we joined a group of fifteen to twenty brothers with their wives at a local restaurant. They were patient when Sandy needed to chronically use the bathroom, was outwardly anxious in waiting for the food to arrive, or was not able to follow the logic of their conversations.

Due to our families living across the country—California, Nevada, Arizona, Texas, Louisiana, Florida, Indiana, Massachusetts, and even Milan, Italy—no one in the family were willing or able to help. Assistance came from private-pay providers. The ad placed in our church bulletin stated the need for a companion. The next week, a woman from the parish, Marilyn, called. She had experience with others who had dementia and could help immediately. During our conversation, I realized that I knew Marilyn. She had been friendly to Sandy for years at various church functions. Marilyn and Sandy bonded immediately, and Marilyn took her out two to three days per week.

Another player on this stage was my friend and ex-supervisor Pat. He had left our agency seven years ago, and he went into the home-health-care field, assisting the sick and elderly. After he left the agency, we lost contact with each other for about two years. I called Pat and explained Sandy's diagnosis. He was very willing to help, and immediately he became a companion with Sandy three days a week.

Sandy and I had friends, Carl and Marie, an elderly couple, who employed a middle-aged, single woman named Dottie for home health care.

They found her private business card in a local gas station. Carl and Marie were very impressed with the quality of Dottie's work and her personality. I contacted Dottie and explained that I needed help with Sandy. Dottie said that she could start immediately and had twenty years of experience helping dementia patients. Always reassuring me that she could assist when I needed her, Sandy and I quickly became her friend. Dottie came to the house two to three times per week to clean, to do the laundry, to give company, and to make dinner. I joked with Dottie, saying, "I lost one wife, and now I'm paying for another!" Dottie worked seven days a week if it meant unselfishly serving her families. With a smile on her face and her belly laugh, she always gave me encouragement.

After Sandy entered the nursing home in January 2015, my goal was to bring her home on weekends. One Monday in March 2015, before I started my twenty-four-hour on-call week for work, I contacted Dottie to see if she could supervise Sandy if I got called out in the middle of the night. As usual, Dottie was willing to help. The next day, Tuesday evening, I received a call from her boyfriend. He stated that Dottie had died in the middle of the night, between 3:00 a.m. and 6:00 a.m. The cause of her death was unknown. Shock consumed me from that day to the present. How can someone so energetic and only in her early fifties pass away? In this painful loss, I ponder that her joyful giving, helpful advice, and hopeful outlook will always give me a script to follow.

During the moderate stage of Sandy's disease, in the spring of 2014, I was encouraged by my support counselor to complete medical and financial power-of-attorney documents with an elder attorney. Having these gave me the right to make decisions for Sandy's medical and financial matters. This was great advice from my counselor, particularly because of the timing. Sandy signed off on these forms just prior to the point where she would not have been able to understand the meaning of them.

The elder attorney possessed great knowledge on the Medicaid process so that Sandy's long-term care could be paid for by the state of Illinois. State law claims that for the disabled one to be eligible for Medicaid, the healthy spouse is allowed to own a car, a house, and no more than a total of $109,000 in cash (checking, savings, IRA, 401K, money market, etc.) In compiling the documentation, Medicaid requires five years of the copies of checking and savings bank statements, tax returns, IRAs, and receipts of withdrawals, deposits, money transfers, money orders, and canceled checks for $1,000 and over. These receipts needed to be placed next to the bank statements (its year and month) that reflected them. Fortunately, I kept diligent records of Sandy's three bank accounts and my four bank accounts. If I had not kept the monthly bank statements from Sandy's bank, the bank would have charged me four dollars per statement; with three accounts per month for five years, this would have cost me $960. Who can afford this? People use Medicaid because they don't have the financial resources for private pay of a facility or they could not afford long-term-care insurance. Medicaid also required paycheck statements, statements of my homeowner's and car-insurance policies, a statement from my life-insurance policy through my employer, proof of bonds, all car titles, real-estate deed, real-estate taxes, and power-of-attorney forms. After I compiled all of the documentation, which took weeks, it filled three three-ring binders.

In January 2015, when Sandy required long-term care, I needed to get down to the ceiling limit in my cash value. This meant spending $7,000 immediately. My elder attorney recommended a prepaid funeral for Sandy. I arranged a meeting with the funeral director, and we wrote out the plan of Sandy's funeral, from giving the family information for the obituary to picking out the cheapest casket in their showroom. Sadness overwhelmed me that one day I would be living out these funeral arrangements.

The End

How? When?

The climactic line in the play of dementia that I need to put into the script is the well-known Serenity Prayer: "Lord, help me to accept the things I cannot change, give me courage to change the things I can, and the wisdom to know the difference." Being a caregiver for Sandy was the most frustrating and sorrowful situation in my life. A benefit from this cross is that it made me humble, bringing me to my knees and saying the Serenity Prayer. In my human nature, and I believe with all humanity, I've always had an inner drive to be happy and have an organized life: in what and where to be educated, in choosing friends, in dating and selecting a spouse, in where to live, in what type of employment to obtain, and in how to plan/manage finances. Putting forth a lot of time and energy to make my life easier and manageable is understandable and acceptable. Now I realize that I should put as much time and energy into building character in order to accept and address unpredictable losses, difficult relationships, and my own mortality. This challenge to face reality takes acceptance, courage, and wisdom.

I never planned for or expected my wife to be stricken with a deadly illness, especially in the early scenes of our marriage. Sandy and I spoke about retiring together, traveling, and caring for each other in our old age. In other words, "making memories" together. What an irony. An old Yiddish saying goes, "Man makes plans, and God laughs." The only plan I really need to make is daily asking God to give me virtue during my journey. A saintly priest from Detroit, Michigan, Venerable Father Solanus Casey, wrote, "Do not pray for an easy life; pray to be stronger people. Do not pray for tasks equal to your powers; pray for powers equal to your task" (Michael Crosby, ed., *Solanus Casey: The Official Account of a Virtuous American Life* [New York: Crossroads Classic, 2000]). Looking back over these past few years—dealing with the unclear diagnosis, lack of support, and Sandy's irritability, obsessions, and loss of intellect and personality—I am amazed that I have continued caring for her despite my anxiety, anger, and depression. This could only have been done by the grace of God. Human love counts the cost; divine love is unselfish and giving. God has given me enough light to deal only with current situations, realizing there is not enough light to continue to the end of the tunnel. Receiving the gift of living in the present prevents the feeling of despair in facing an unknown future, and it teaches trust that God has always provided and will provide. We have heard the common sayings "One day at a time," "Live in the moment," and "Let go and let God." These statements on the surface seem trite and cliché, but when I applied them as a caregiver, they came to life.

Dementia literature depressingly explains that this disease is "progressive," meaning the symptoms of one's life's functioning only decline, and nobody recovers from it. As a caregiver, I could only manage (not cure) this disease, provide the daily care Sandy needed, and continue the process of grieving the loss of my wife and best friend. Dementia is called "the long good-bye" because the person I have known is step-by-step fading away, and death is the only conclusion. The unknown is *how long* it will take one to fully pass away. My father, within two months, went from dancing with the nurses at the memory clinic to refusing to eat any of his meals. He was placed on hospice for ten days and then died. Each day I spent with Sandy,

I treated her as if this was her last. As caregivers, we fulfill our loving role throughout all of the various acts in the dementia play, even until the curtain on the loved one's life closes.

"All the world's a stage." Caregivers have their entrances, and those cared for only have exits. "Play on" until the close of the last scene. Then we shall hear from within ourselves, from others, and from our God a resounding, "Bravo! Well done!"

Epilogue

It Ain't Over Until It's Over

D ecember 2015: My book was in the final-corrections stage and ready to seek a publisher. Then the unthinkable happened.

On December 23, 2015 (an *un*merry Christmas) at 8:30 p.m., I entered the community room at the nursing home/memory clinic to pick up Sandy for the Christmas weekend. She glanced at me and turned her head away. Normally, she was filled with excitement in greeting me and was eager to leave the building, but now, she displayed apathy toward my presence. The CNA (certified nursing assistant) who was sitting with Sandy stated that about ten minutes earlier, Sandy started to act odd, becoming distant to others and moving her right arm straight out in a waving motion. I noticed her glassy eyes and a flat affect. Sandy stated my name, but there was no interest in making conversation or exiting with me to go home. We asked if Sandy was tired and wanted to go to bed. She said yes. Attempting to stand, she stumbled onto her right leg, and the CNA caught her from falling. A wheelchair was necessary to get to the bedroom. Earlier this day, Sandy had been pacing up and down the halls, as she normally does, and she even attempted to flee the facility with another resident.

At 8:40 p.m., the CNA called for the nurse to do a medical examination. She examined Sandy for a possible stroke. Her pupils were not dilated, hand strength was equal, facial features were even, and her vitals were normal. The nursing-home doctor concluded that it was not a stroke and recommended that Sandy go to bed and be monitored every hour. The medical staff thought that it might be a UTI (urinary-tract infection) since normally dementia patients act distant when they have an infection or virus.

Christmas Eve day, Sandy continued to act fatigued and strange. When I took her to the bathroom, she went around the backside of the door and started rubbing the hinges. The staff continued to check her vitals, which were normal.

On Christmas Day, while I was driving to the facility to give Sandy her holiday gifts, the nurse called my cell phone and said that Sandy was going to be admitted to the emergency room. She had showed no change in her strange behavior, and now her blood pressure was high. I was thankful for this decision because I had been perplexed about her medical issues for the past two days. At the ER, the first doctor examined her for a stroke and said, "I put my vote on a UTI, but I am going to order a CT scan of the brain anyway." I agreed, thinking that hospitals tend to be overly cautious anyway.

When the results came back, the next shift doctor read the results. He stated that Sandy had suffered an acute stroke to the left base of the brain and that the nursing home was not qualified to diagnose whether a resident had a stroke. After detailed questions about the sequence of events on the evening of December 23, he announced, with controlled anger, that if Sandy had come to the ER within the first four hours of the stroke, the hospital could have unclogged it with medication. At this moment, I almost passed out from shock and panic. Sandy was now having trouble standing and walking. She either shook her head for "yes" or "no" or gave one-word answers. When she could create a sentence, its content was disconnected and random. Besides being frequently fatigued, she lost the ability to feed herself and use the bathroom. Although the nursing-home medical staff was seemingly fooled, the doctor said that the stroke exam they performed only rules out 90 percent of stroke types. The one Sandy had could only be diagnosed with a CT scan. They should have erred on the side of caution and admitted her to the hospital at 8:41 p.m. on December 23.

The irony in managing Sandy's behaviors was displayed on December 30. Sandy and I had a three-month follow-up appointment with the neurologist. I had planned to ask for medication to help reduce Sandy's constant need to be on the go when she came home on weekends. The ability to relax at home or in the community was minimal—for example, a few minutes after ordering our food in a restaurant, Sandy would question where the entree was, insisting on walking into the kitchen and inquiring about it. Or once we pulled into our driveway after grocery shopping, getting gas, paying bills, picking up laundry, and eating at a restaurant, Sandy would say, "We're going inside the house, turning around, and getting out of here." The optimal activities that kept her calm were watching TV, which could be up to an hour, running errands, or riding in the car. The stroke changed her personality from being an overly hyper and anxious five-year-old to being an extremely passive and sedate one-year-old. In regard to the neurologist appointment, it was cancelled. No medication was now necessary due to the stroke-induced lethargy. Be careful what you wish for.

At the end of Sandy's hospital stay, the doctor recommended physical, occupational, and speech therapy. He concluded that we would not know how much she could progress for three to four months. The neurologist stated that the stroke had no correlation with the dementia. Being at the hospital half of Christmas Day, I did not have a chance to eat. About 9:00 p.m., since no restaurants were open, I had my Christmas dinner at a Shell gas station: a holiday banquet of a cold sandwich, chips, and a Coke. Three days after the hospitalization, Sandy was discharged and admitted back into her nursing home, commencing and continuing with all of the therapies.

While I was crying in despair and questioning if I could continue caring for Sandy during this act of the dementia play, my counselor recalled that true love is in the intellect (knowing what's good) and in the will (choosing and acting on the good) and not in the emotional reactions or feelings. She also reminded me I was able to manage past crises and that God would give me the fortitude again to handle this one; there is no reason to doubt. Therefore, I "play on," asking for the grace to be strong, to love, and to serve the needs of my wife.

"Love is patient, love is kind. It does not envy, it does not boast, it is not proud. It does not dishonor others, it is not self-seeking, it is not easily angered, it keeps no record of wrongs. Love does not delight in evil but rejoices with the truth. It always protects, always trusts, always hopes, always perseveres. Love never fails."

—1 CORINTHIANS 13:4–8

My parents celebrating their fifty-fifth wedding anniversary

Sandy and I as newlyweds

Made in the USA
Lexington, KY
14 December 2017